EDMONTON OILERS

BY TED COLEMAN

Book design by Maggie Villaume
Cover design by Maggie Villaume

Photographs ©: Jason Franson/The Canadian Press/AP Images, cover, 29; Brett Holmes/Icon Sportswire, 4–5, 7, 8; Richard Drew/AP Images, 10–11; Bruce Bennett/Getty Images, 13; Bob Doeppers/Indianapolis Star News/AP Images, 15; Ray Stubblebine/AP Images, 16–17; Dave Buston/ The Canadian Press/AP Images, 19; Ray Giguere/The Canadian Press/AP Images, 21; Wa Funches/AP Images, 22–23; Charles Krupa/AP Images, 24–25; Tom Gannam/AP Images, 27

Press Box Books, an imprint of Press Room Editions.

ISBN
978-1-63494-593-6 (library bound)
978-1-63494-611-7 (paperback)
978-1-63494-646-9 (epub)
978-1-63494-629-2 (hosted ebook)

Library of Congress Control Number: 2022912826

Distributed by North Star Editions, Inc.
2297 Waters Drive
Mendota Heights, MN 55120
www.northstareditions.com

Printed in the United States of America
Mankato, MN
012023

ABOUT THE AUTHOR

Ted Coleman is a sportswriter who lives in Louisville, Kentucky, with his trusty Affenpinscher, Chloe.

TABLE OF CONTENTS

1

Connor McDavid lines up a shot in the 2022 playoffs against the Calgary Flames.

MCDAVID MAGIC

The Edmonton Oilers had not made the conference finals in 17 years. Now they had a chance to change that. The Oilers had a 3–1 series lead over their biggest rivals, the Calgary Flames, in the 2022 playoffs. And they had a chance to clinch the series in Calgary.

The series had been high scoring. There were 36 goals scored in the first four games.

Game 5 was no different. After the second period, the game was tied 4–4. But neither team scored in the third period. The game would be decided in overtime.

Edmonton had an advantage. Connor McDavid and Leon Draisaitl were two of the National Hockey League's (NHL's) best offensive players. McDavid's 123 points led the NHL that season. The speedy center had already tallied 11 points in the first four games against Calgary. One more would send Edmonton to the next round.

Five minutes passed in overtime. The Oilers dumped the puck into their offensive zone. Flames defender Noah Hanifin got to it first. As he skated away

Leon Draisaitl's 110 points were the fourth-most in the NHL in 2021–22.

with it, McDavid made his move. He quickly cut off Hanifin. Then he lifted Hanifin's stick. The puck was loose. Draisaitl got to it first. While being pressed

McDavid slides on the ice celebrating his series-winning goal against the Flames.

against the boards, Draisaitl passed it back to McDavid on top of the face-off circle. Before the Flames could react, McDavid snapped a wrist shot on goal.

The puck whizzed by the goalie's glove and into the net.

McDavid slid on his knees in celebration. His teammates mobbed him on the boards. It was McDavid's first playoff overtime goal in his career. Edmonton's biggest star delivered in the biggest moment. And the Oilers were headed to the conference finals for the first time since 2006.

DYNAMIC DUO

Connor McDavid and Leon Draisaitl each played 16 games in the 2022 playoffs. McDavid tallied 33 points, the most in the playoffs and one more than Draisaitl. But Draisaitl was the main man against the Flames. He recorded 15 assists over those five games. That set a record for most assists in a single playoff series.

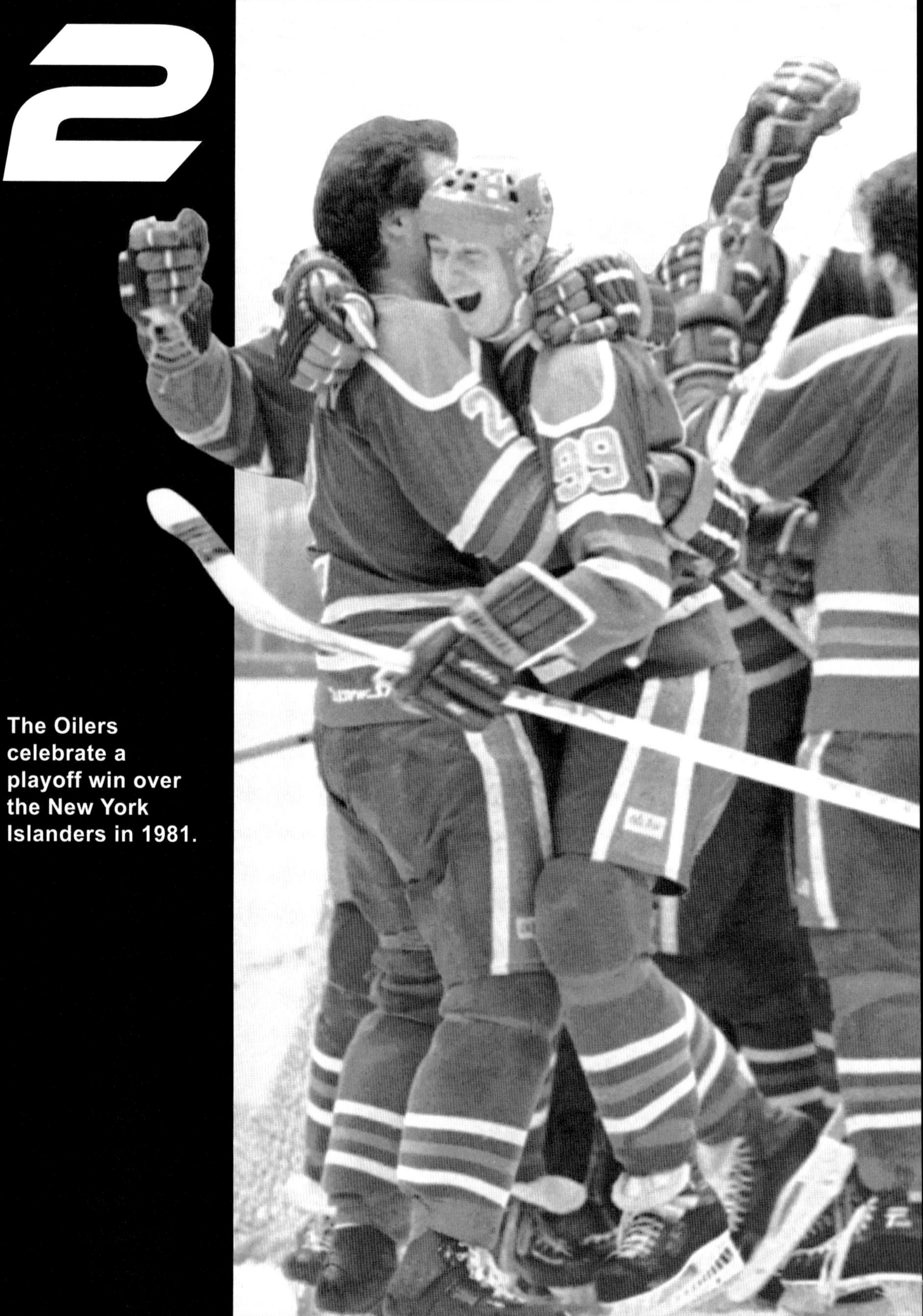

2

The Oilers celebrate a playoff win over the New York Islanders in 1981.

WHA YEARS

Hockey has been a popular sport in Edmonton for a long time. The city's first pro hockey team formed in the early 1900s. The NHL did not yet exist. But the best Canadian teams were already battling for the Stanley Cup. Teams from Edmonton challenged for the Stanley Cup in 1908 and 1910. But they lost both times.

However, no Edmonton team lasted long. The Oilers looked to

change that. The team formed in 1972 as the Alberta Oilers. The Oilers were members of the World Hockey Association (WHA). The WHA included 12 teams across Canada and the United States.

The Oilers were named for Alberta because they planned to play in both Edmonton and Calgary. But that never happened. The team played its first season in Edmonton. Then it took that city's name for the 1973–74 season.

WHAT'S AN OILER?

The Oilers took their name from another hockey team, the Edmonton Oil Kings. Oilers owner "Wild Bill" Hunter also owned the Oil Kings. Both teams' names are in reference to the oil industry in Alberta. The team's logo includes an oil drop and letters that appear to be dripping.

Al Hamilton played in Edmonton for eight seasons from 1972 to 1980.

The WHA became famous for attracting NHL stars. Legends Bobby Hull and Gordie Howe each played in the WHA. The Oilers never had stars of that level. But they did have plenty of fan favorites, such as defenseman Al Hamilton.

Hamilton was the team's first captain. Over the years he battled through injuries. Hamilton was never the most talented player in the league. But fans admired the effort he gave every night.

The Oilers had little success in the WHA. They usually made the playoffs. However, the team rarely advanced. That changed with the help of just one teenager.

Wayne Gretzky had been a youth hockey prodigy. The NHL didn't allow teenagers. But in 1978, the 17-year-old Gretzky was tearing it up for the Indianapolis Racers in the WHA. Needing money, the Racers traded Gretzky to the Oilers that November.

Wayne Gretzky played eight games with the Indianapolis Racers before joining the Oilers.

He scored 110 points in 80 games as a rookie. The Oilers reached the WHA championship series. And Gretzky was just getting started.

Wayne Gretzky led the NHL in scoring in eight of his nine seasons in Edmonton.

GLORY YEARS

new era began for the Oilers in 1979–80. Edmonton and three other WHA teams joined the NHL. That unleashed Wayne Gretzky on the world's best league.

Gretzky was still only 18. Yet he was already a superstar. His 137 points tied for the league lead. That earned him the Hart Memorial Trophy as the league's Most Valuable Player (MVP).

Gretzky helped turn the Oilers into one of the NHL's best teams.

The 1983–84 Oilers featured three 50-goal scorers. That had never happened in NHL history. Gretzky had 87 goals. Glenn Anderson scored 54. And Jari Kurri added 52. Then there was Mark Messier. The tough center was a future Hart Trophy winner himself.

The Oilers lost the 1983 Stanley Cup Final to the New York Islanders. In 1984 the teams met again. This time the Oilers broke through. Messier won the Conn Smythe Trophy, given to the MVP of the playoffs.

Kurri was at his best in the 1985 playoffs. He tied an NHL record with

Mark Messier smiles with the Conn Smythe Trophy in 1984.

19 goals. Defenseman Paul Coffey could score like a forward. He had 12 goals and 25 assists in those playoffs. But it was

Gretzky who won the Conn Smythe. He tallied a playoff record 47 points. This time the Oilers knocked off the Philadelphia Flyers in the Cup Final.

The Oilers could not make it three championships in a row. But they managed four in five years. They beat the Flyers in 1987. Then they defeated the Boston Bruins in 1988.

Everything changed 11 weeks later. Owner Peter Pocklington was worried

A NICE TRY

The Oilers' first Stanley Cup meant a great deal to Oilers owner Peter Pocklington. As a tribute to his father, Basil, he had his name engraved on the Stanley Cup. But Basil had no role on the team. When the NHL found out, they ordered that Basil's name be stamped out with 16 Xs. That was the first time that had been done to a name on the Cup.

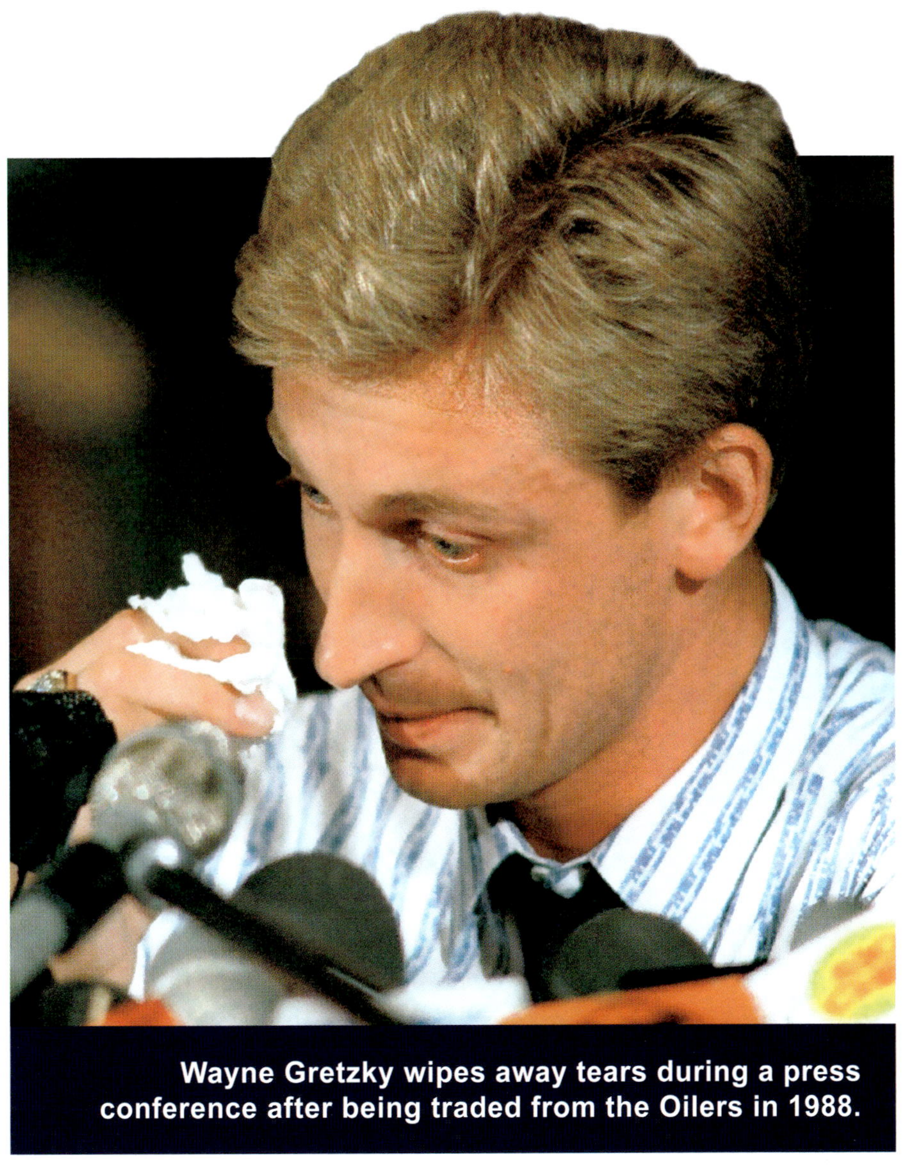

Wayne Gretzky wipes away tears during a press conference after being traded from the Oilers in 1988.

Gretzky would not sign a new contract. He wanted to get something in return. So he traded Gretzky to the Los Angeles Kings. That move shocked the hockey world.

WAYNE GRETZKY

As an 11-year-old in 1971–72, Wayne Gretzky scored 378 goals in 85 games. He quickly began moving up. His scoring numbers hardly slowed. Gretzky wore uniform No. 9 growing up. He did that as a tribute to fellow No. 9 Gordie Howe, known as "Mr. Hockey." Gretzky ended up breaking most of Howe's records. But he did it in No. 99. Gretzky switched after a year in which No. 9 was already taken.

Gretzky's scoring numbers were incredible. He led the league in scoring 11 times. He won nine Hart Trophies. And he broke the biggest record hockey has to offer. He smashed Howe's record of 801 career goals with 894. Of those, 583 came during his nine NHL seasons in Edmonton.

Gretzky was not a big player. But he used his skating to get open and create chances. It was why he was known simply as "The Great One."

Wayne Gretzky battles for a puck in a 1988 game against the New York Islanders.

4

Craig MacTavish celebrates a teammate's goal in Game 1 of the 1990 Stanley Cup Final.

STRIKING OIL

Losing the best player in the world was hard for fans to take. It got worse in the 1989 playoffs. The Oilers faced the Los Angeles Kings in the first round. Wayne Gretzky led all players in points as the Kings won the series.

But Mark Messier, Glenn Anderson, and Jari Kurri kept Edmonton among the NHL's best. In the 1990 playoffs, the Oilers turned the tables. They swept Gretzky and the Kings in the second round.

Goalie Bill Ranford started the season as Grant Fuhr's backup. But Fuhr got hurt and Ranford was in. He dominated the Boston Bruins in the 1990 Stanley Cup Final. Ranford won the Conn Smythe as the Oilers were champs again.

The 1990 Cup was the last in Edmonton's glory years. Key players soon retired or left the team. By 1993 the Oilers were out of the playoffs. In 1998 they nearly moved to Texas before local buyers saved the team.

By 2005–06 the Oilers hadn't won a playoff series since 1998. But defenseman Chris Pronger and forward Michael Peca

Chris Pronger tallied a team-high 21 points during the 2006 playoffs.

helped change that. They led the Oilers to the Stanley Cup Final that year. But they lost to the Carolina Hurricanes.

The Oilers didn't make the playoffs again until 2017. All that losing meant they got high draft picks. From 2010 to 2012 the Oilers chose first overall each year. But none of the picks helped them turn it around.

The Oilers finally nailed the first overall pick in 2015. Center Connor McDavid was a superstar right away. He led the league in points in his second season. And the Oilers were back in the playoffs. He and Leon Draisaitl, the 2014

OUTDOOR HOCKEY

The NHL's outdoor Winter Classic is now a yearly tradition. Back in 2003, the Oilers hosted the first outdoor game in league history. They played the Montreal Canadiens in a football stadium. More than 57,000 fans showed up. The Oilers lost 4–3.

Connor McDavid (left) and Leon Draisaitl celebrate a goal against the New York Rangers in a 2021 game.

third overall pick, formed a powerful scoring duo.

Many fans believed McDavid was the best player since Gretzky. Only time would tell if he could also bring a Stanley Cup to Edmonton.

EDMONTON OILERS QUICK STATS

TEAM HISTORY: Alberta Oilers (1972–73), Edmonton Oilers (1973–)

STANLEY CUP CHAMPIONSHIPS: 5 (1984, 1985, 1987, 1988, 1990)

KEY COACHES:

- Glen Sather (1976–89, 1993–94): 464 wins, 268 losses, 110 ties
- Craig MacTavish (2000–09): 301 wins, 252 losses, 47 ties, 56 overtime losses

HOME ARENA: Rogers Place (Edmonton, AB)

MOST CAREER POINTS: Wayne Gretzky (1,669)

MOST CAREER GOALS: Wayne Gretzky (583)

MOST CAREER ASSISTS: Wayne Gretzky (1,086)

MOST CAREER SHUTOUTS: Tommy Salo (23)

**Stats are accurate through the 2021–22 season.*

GLOSSARY

CAPTAIN
A team's leader.

CONTRACT
A written agreement that keeps a player with a team for a certain amount of time.

DRAFT
An event that allows teams to choose new players coming into the league.

ERA
A period of time in history.

POINT
A statistic that a player earns by scoring a goal or having an assist.

PRODIGY
A person who is extremely talented at a young age.

ROOKIE
A professional athlete in his or her first year of competition.

TO LEARN MORE

BOOKS

Doeden, Matt. *G.O.A.T. Hockey Teams*. Minneapolis, MN: Lerner Publications, 2021.

Fishman, Jon M. *Hockey's G.O.A.T.: Wayne Gretzky, Sidney Crosby, and More*. Minneapolis, MN: Lerner Publications, 2020.

Price, Karen. *Connor McDavid: Hockey Superstar*. Mendota Heights, MN: Press Box Books, 2019.

WEBSITES

To learn more about the Edmonton Oilers, go to **pressboxbooks.com/AllAccess**.

These links are routinely monitored and updated to provide the most current information available.

INDEX